Adventures in Canadian History

THE DEATH OF TECUMSEH

Books for Younger Readers by Pierre Berton

The Golden Trail
The Secret World of Og

PIERRE BERTON

The Battles of the War of · 1812 ·

THE DEATH OF TECUMSEH

ILLUSTRATIONS BY PAUL MC CUSKER

M&S

An M&S Paperback from
McClelland & Stewart Inc.
The Canadian Publishers

An M&S Paperback Original from McClelland & Stewart Inc.

Copyright © 1994 by Pierre Berton Enterprises Ltd.

Canadian Cataloguing in Publication Data

Berton, Pierre, 1920-
The death of Tecumseh

(Adventures in Canadian history. Battles of the War of 1812)
An M&S paperback original.
Includes index.

ISBN 0-7710-1423-6

1. Thames River (Ont.), Battle of, 1813 – Juvenile literature.   2. Tecumseh, 1768?-1813 – Death and burial – Juvenile literature.   3. Canada – History – War of 1812 – Campaigns – Juvenile literature.*   4. Northwest, Old – History – War of 1812 – Campaigns – Juvenile literature.   5. United States – History – War of 1812 – Campaigns – Juvenile literature.   6. Canada – History – War of 1812 – Participation, Indian – Juvenile literature.*   7. Indians of North America – Ontario – Juvenile literature.   I. McCusker, Paul.   II. Title.   III. Series: Berton, Pierre, 1920-   . Adventures in Canadian history. The battles at the War of 1812.

E3S6.T3B47 1994   j971.03'4   C94-931179-0

Series design by Tania Craan
Cover and text design by Stephen Kenny
Cover illustration by Scott Cameron
Interior illustrations by Paul McCusker
Maps by James Loates
Editor: Peter Carver

Typesetting by M&S

The support of the Government of Ontario through the Ministry of Culture, Tourism and Recreation is acknowledged.

Printed and bound in Canada by Webcom Limited

McClelland & Stewart Inc.
The Canadian Publishers
481 University Avenue
Toronto, Ontario
M5G 2E9

1 2 3 4 5   98 97 96 95 94

Contents

Map appears on page 12.

The events in this book actually happened as told here. Nothing has been made up. This is a work of non-fiction and there is archival evidence for every story and, indeed, every remark made in this book.

Adventures in Canadian History

THE DEATH OF TECUMSEH

Tecumseh (foreground) with Henry Procter (left) and William Henry Harrison.

Chapter One
The Shawnee's dream

TECUMSEH! THAT NAME ECHOES DOWN the corridors of history – as well it might. Of all the great native leaders on both sides of the Canada-U.S. border, he is without doubt the greatest.

A master strategist, his handling of his native followers helped General Isaac Brock capture Detroit in the summer of 1812. (See *The Capture of Detroit* in this series.)

A brilliant orator, he could bring tears to the eyes of white men who did not understand a word he said.

A compassionate leader, he was opposed to the ritual killing or torture of prisoners.

A champion of his people, his dream was to unite the various tribes who occupied American territory and to form an independent native state.

This is the story of Tecumseh's last brave days in the second year of the War of 1812. But the beginnings of the story go back to the Battle of Tippecanoe in 1811 (described in *Revenge of the Tribes* in this series).

Tecumseh – a muscular Shawnee with golden skin and hazel eyes – had every reason to hate the Americans. They were driving his people farther and farther west, stealing native land. When Tecumseh and his mystic brother, the Prophet, tried to set up an independent community called Prophet's Town on the Wabash (in what is now Indiana), his old nemesis, William Henry Harrison, governor of Indiana Territory, attacked and destroyed it.

It was this attack, the Battle of Tippecanoe, that caused Tecumseh to gather his followers and cross the border into Canada. For years he had dreamed an ancient dream of a confederacy which would unite the tribes and set up a native state in the heart of North America. We can see his passion and his commitment in a rare published report of a speech he made in 1806:

"It is true I am Shawnee. My forefathers were warriors. Their son is a warrior. From them I take only my existence. From my tribe I take nothing. I am the maker of my own fortune. And oh!, that I might make that of my red people, and of my country, as great as the conceptions of my mind, when I think of the Spirit that rules the universe....

"The way, and the only way, to check and stop this evil, is for all the red men to unite in claiming a common and equal right in the land; as it was at first; and should be yet; for it never was divided, but belongs to us all, for the use of each. That no part has a right to sell, even to each other, much less to strangers who want it all and will not do with less....

"Sell a country! Why not sell the air, the clouds, and the great sea, as well as the earth? Did not the Great Spirit make them all for the use of his children?"

At Tippecanoe, Harrison, hungry for Indian land, determined to stop any attempt by the Shawnee chief to form such a confederacy, and while he destroyed the community, he could not shatter Tecumseh's dream.

Harrison's senseless destruction of Prophet's Town drove the Shawnee and his followers – representing a dozen tribes – into the arms of the British and Canadians. When war broke out the following June, Tecumseh was determined to fight against the Americans. And so, in trying to stop the formation of an Indian confederacy, Harrison had succeeded in strengthening Tecumseh's plans.

In the summer of 1812, the British, Canadians, and Indians hurled back every American attempt to invade Canada. But now, as our story begins, in September 1813, the tide was turning.

Tecumseh's old enemy, Harrison, was on the march following the American victory in the Battle of Lake Erie earlier that summer. (See *The Battle of Lake Erie* in this series.) All the British ships were sunk or lost in that lake battle, and Erie was now in American hands. Their vessels could cruise those waters at will, landing soldiers anywhere.

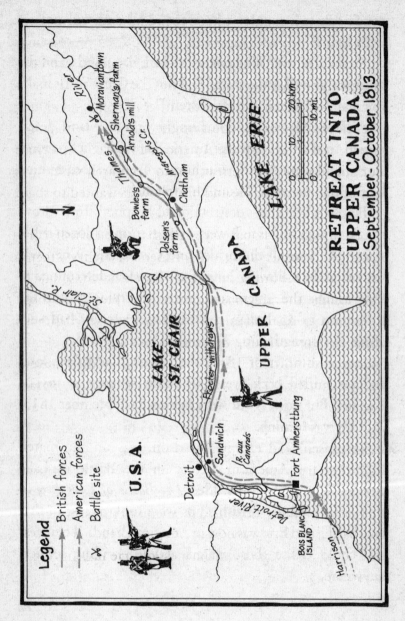

Legend

- → British forces
- ⇢ American forces
- ⚔ Battle site

U.S.A.

Detroit

LAKE ST. CLAIR

St. Clair R.

LAKE ERIE

Sandwich

Procter withdraws

R. aux Canards

Fort Amherstburg

Bois Blanc Island

Detroit River

Harrison

UPPER CANADA

Dolsen's farm

Bowles's farm

Chatham

McGregor's Cr.

Thames

Arnold's mill

Sherman's farm

Moraviantown

River

RETREAT INTO UPPER CANADA
September–October 1813

0 10 20 km

0 10 mi.

The British could not hope to hold the American territory that Brock and Tecumseh had captured the previous summer. Detroit would have to be evacuated. Amherstburg, on the Canadian side, was threatened.

The British had two choices: either to stand and fight at the water's edge or to retreat up the valley of the Thames, dig in, and try to stop the American advance. The British command wanted to retreat, but to Tecumseh retreat was out of the question. He and his followers wanted to stand and fight.

Tecumseh must have wished that the British commander at Amherstburg, Major General Henry Procter, had some of the brilliance of Isaac Brock, at whose side he had fought the previous summer. But Brock had been killed at Queenston Heights. And Procter lacked Brock's drive, his sense of leadership, and his easy way with his men. He was in his fiftieth year, a good enough soldier, but not very imaginative. There was a heaviness about him, his face was fleshy, and his body tended toward fat. He was "one of the meanest looking men I ever saw," in the words of an American colonel.

Procter had three failings: he couldn't make up his mind quickly, as good leaders must; he kept his plans to himself without telling others; and, in moments of stress, he tended to panic.

Tecumseh was in a violent passion. He had just come over the lake from Detroit, which the British, to his fury, had decided to abandon. Now it looked as if Procter was also trying to retreat from Amherstburg.

Procter, as usual, was being secretive. He insisted, against all evidence, that the British had won the lake battle! That further angered Tecumseh. The Shawnee was no fool and didn't like to be treated as one. He had been quarreling with Procter since Brock's death. In Tecumseh's view, Brock was a *man*, whereas Procter was only fit to wear women's clothes. And now here he was, a British general, afraid to face his Shawnee ally with the truth.

We cannot blame Tecumseh for being disillusioned. He had, since 1809, been an optimist, convinced that he could somehow gather the various tribes into a mighty union. By helping the British, he thought, they would be able to hold onto their hunting grounds and their traditional way of life.

But the war had gone sour. Tecumseh had just come back to Canada from the south, where he had tried to convince the other tribes to join him. He had failed. He was still obsessed with a single goal, but that goal now seemed to be in doubt, and Tecumseh was close to despair.

He told his followers that the king over the water had broken his promise to them. The British had pledged that there would be plenty of white men to fight along with the Indians. But where were they?

"The number," said Tecumseh, "is not now greater than at the commencement of the war; we are treated by them like the dogs of snipe hunters; we are always sent ahead to *start the game*; it is better that we should return to our country and let the Americans come and fight the British."

Many of Tecumseh's people agreed. But the Sioux, and their one-time enemies, the Chippewa, who had come over to the British side, persuaded him to remain.

Now, with Fort Detroit being dismantled, Tecumseh had further evidence of Procter's distrust. Off he went in a fury to the home of Matthew Elliott of the Indian Department at Amherstburg, who cringed under Tecumseh's fury. Tecumseh warned Elliott that, if Procter retreated, his followers would make a public spectacle. He threatened to bring out the great wampum belt that was a symbol of British-Indian friendship and cut it in two to indicate eternal separation. Worse, Tecumseh warned, the Indians would fall on the British Army, which they outnumbered three to one, and cut the British to pieces.

Retreat was not in Tecumseh's makeup. He believed only in attack. His one goal was to kill as many of the enemy as possible. Now in his mid-forties, he had been fighting white Americans all his life to prevent them moving into land that had always been native territory.

There was no love lost between the Kentucky frontiersmen and the Indians. The whites were moving westward, seizing the land as their own; the Shawnee were engaged in a vain attempt to stop them. At the age of fifteen, Tecumseh was fighting Kentuckians. At sixteen, he was ambushing their boats. At twenty-two, he was serving as a raider and scout against the United States, which sided with the white frontiersmen.

When his elder brother was killed, Tecumseh became band leader in his stead, going north again to take part in the disastrous Battle of Fallen Timbers. There, in August 1794, not far from the present site of Toledo, Ohio, General "Mad Anthony" Wayne attacked and destroyed the Northwest Indian Confederacy, ending the natives' attempt to retain their land. Three thousand Americans destroyed a force of 1,400 natives. Most of the present state of Ohio and parts of Indiana, Illinois, and Michigan were lost to the tribes, which included the Shawnee.

On that black day, Tecumseh, his musket jammed, tried vainly to rally his followers, waving a useless weapon as they scattered before the American bayonets. Tecumseh was a man who didn't believe in holding back, but now his British allies wanted him to do just that.

Chapter Two

"I feel I shall never return"

ONCE AGAIN TECUMSEH WAS FACING HIS OLD enemy, William Henry Harrison. On more than one occasion he had used his golden voice to frustrate Harrison's hunger for Indian lands. Now Harrison had Lake Erie to himself and could land anywhere.

Harrison had a score to settle with Tecumseh, who had frustrated his land grab. But Tecumseh had a score to settle with Harrison, who had destroyed the capital of his confederacy in the Battle of Tippecanoe. He could not wait to get at the general, and he used the weapon of his oratory to rally his people and to blackmail the British into standing fast.

On the morning of September 14 – just four days after the Americans won the Battle of Lake Erie – he summoned his followers at Amherstburg. They squatted in their hundreds on the fort's parade ground as he strode over to a large stone on the riverbank. It was here that announcements of importance were made, and here that Tecumseh

Tecumseh makes an impassioned speech at Amherstburg.

made the last speech of his life. It was addressed to Procter, who was standing nearby with a group of officers.

First Tecumseh spoke of his suspicions, born of long experience going back to the peace that followed the American Revolution:

"Father, listen. Our fleet has gone out, we know they have fought. We have heard the great guns, but know nothing of what has happened to our father with one arm. [A reference to Captain Robert Barclay, commander of the British fleet.] Our ships have gone one way and we are much astonished to see our father tying up everything and preparing to run the other, without letting his children know what his intentions are.

"You always told us to remain here and take care of our land.... You always told us you would never draw your foot off British ground. But now, Father, we see that you are drawing back, and we are sorry to see our father doing so without seeing the enemy. We must compare our father's conduct to a fat animal that carries its tail upon its back. But when affrighted, it drops it between its legs and runs off."

He urged Procter to stay and fight any attempted invasion. If Procter was defeated, Tecumseh promised he would remain on the British side and retreat with the troops. If Procter wouldn't fight, the Indians would:

"Father, you have got the arms and ammunition.... If you have any idea of going away, give them to us.... Our lives are in the hands of the Great Spirit; we are determined to defend our land; and if it is his will, we wish to leave our bones upon it."

With these words, some of his people leapt up prepared to attack the British immediately if their leader gave the word. But they did not act, because Procter promised to hold a council with the tribesmen two days later.

Procter was faced with a serious problem. His fort was defenceless. He had stripped it of its cannon to arm one of the big ships now captured by the Americans. A third of the troops had also been lost to him in that battle. He was out of provisions. The new supplies would have to be sent overland because they could no longer move by water, which the Americans controlled.

What's more, Harrison had a strong attack force and also the means to get across the lake unmolested and into Canada. Procter's own men were battle weary, starving, and in despair over the loss of the fleet.

Procter was not daring. He had often opposed the bold Isaac Brock, who had captured Detroit in a single thrust. Procter had been against that. He was a man who went by the book, and, in doing so, often wasted precious time.

The British felt they had reason to withdraw from Fort Amherstburg. With the lake battle lost, they knew that Harrison could land troops anywhere along the north shore of Lake Erie and get around the British to take them from the rear. But if Procter moved up the Thames Valley, Harrison's supply lines would be stretched to the limit.

Harrison's army was composed mainly of volunteers

who had signed on for only six months. After that term was up, experience showed that most of them would hightail it back to their farms in the United States.

But if Procter was to move, he would have to move at once, for Harrison would be at his heels, giving him no chance to prepare a defence. There, Procter showed his hesitancy. A week went by and nothing happened. Then at last he held his promised meeting with the tribesmen.

Here was his problem: ten thousand native women and children would have to be brought across the lake and moved up the Thames Valley ahead of the army, together with those white settlers who didn't wish to remain under foreign rule. The sick would also have to be removed, and that would be awkward. Furthermore, they would have to take all the military stores with them – a cumbersome business.

This was an enormous undertaking. It required drive, organizational ability, decision, and a sense of urgency – qualities that Procter didn't have.

Indeed, this evacuation posed as many problems for Procter as did the advancing American forces. Harrison was not encumbered by thousands of natives and civilians clogging the narrow trails along the Thames.

Procter met the Indians on September 18. Again Tecumseh urged that Harrison be allowed to land and march on Amherstburg. He and his Indians were prepared to attack on the American flank, with the British facing the front. If the attack failed, Tecumseh said, he would make a stand at River aux Canards, three miles (4.8 km) north of Amherstburg. He had defended it successfully the previous year, when an American force had earlier tried to invade Canada.

Procter rejected the plan. Tecumseh, in a fury, called him "a miserable old squaw." At that the chiefs leapt up, brandishing tomahawks, their yells echoing down from the vaulted roof of the lofty council chamber.

Finally Procter abandoned the secrecy that had caused so much trouble up to this point. He unrolled a map and explained his position. He pointed out that if gunboats came up the Detroit River they could cut off the Indians camped on the American side. That would make it impossible for them to help the British. It would allow Harrison to move to the mouth of the Thames River and attack the British from the rear, cutting off all retreat.

Tecumseh considered this carefully. He asked some questions and made some shrewd remarks. He had never seen a map like this before. This part of the country was new to him, but he quickly saw the significance of the problems the British faced.

Procter promised to make a stand near the community of Chatham, at the forks of the Thames River. He said he would fortify the position and would "mix our bones with [your] bones." Tecumseh asked for time to confer with his fellow chiefs. He managed to convince them to reverse their own stand and follow him up a river unknown to them and into a foreign country. But Tecumseh still had doubts.

On September 23 the British destroyed Fort Amherstburg, wrecking the dockyards and burning all the public buildings. The army set off for Sandwich (near the present city of Windsor), directly across from Detroit. "We are going to follow the British," Tecumseh remarked sadly, "and I feel that I shall never return."

British forces withdraw from Fort Amherstburg.

Chapter Three

"We must not retreat"

THE BRITISH WITHDRAWAL MOVED AT A snail's pace. It took ten days just to get all the stores and baggage a few miles up the Detroit River by wagon and scow. The townspeople insisted on bringing their personal belongings – an unnecessary burden that tied up the boats and caused a delay in moving the women, children, and the sick.

The military stores were in a snarl. Entrenching tools, for instance, which should have been carried with the troops, were placed at the bottom of the boats, and so were difficult to reach when the soldiers needed them.

Finally, on September 27, the British destroyed the barracks and public buildings at Detroit. The rearguard moved across the river. The rest of the troops marched out of Sandwich.

That same evening, Jacques Bâby, a prominent merchant and a lieutenant-colonel in the militia, gave a dinner for the senior officers of the 41st Regiment in his stone mansion at Sandwich. Tecumseh attended wearing deerskin trousers, a calico shirt, and a red cloak. He was in a black mood, eating with pistols on each side of his plate, his hunting knife in front of him.

A knock came at the door. A British scout announced that the enemy fleet had entered the river and was sailing north near Amherstburg. Tecumseh rose, his hands on his pistols, and turned to General Procter.

"Father, we must go to meet the enemy.... We must not retreat.... If you take us from this post you will lead us far, far away ... tell us Goodbye forever and leave us to the mercy of the Long Knives. I tell you I am sorry I have listened to you thus far, for if we remained at the town ... we could have kept the enemy from landing and have held our hunting grounds for our children.

"Now they tell me you want to withdraw to the river Thames.... I am tired of it all. Every word you say evaporates like the smoke from our pipes. Father, you are like the crawfish that does not know how to walk straight ahead."

Procter did not reply, and the dinner broke up. Tecumseh had no choice but to follow the British with those warriors who were still loyal to his cause. But many were not. His force now numbered no more than one thousand. The Ottawa and Chippewa bands had already sent three warriors to make peace with Harrison. The Wyandot, Miami, and some Delaware were about to do the same. In 1812 these tribesmen had been necessary for a victory. Without them Upper Canada would have become an American state. Now Procter saw them only as a nuisance.

In the days that followed, the British general seemed unable to make any decision. Procter literally failed to burn his bridges behind him to delay Harrison. He believed that if he did so the Indians would think themselves cut off and abandon his cause. He purposely held back the army to wait for the Indians. Aware of his pledge to Tecumseh to make a stand at the forks of the Thames, he dashed ahead to look over the ground. He left his second-in-command, Lieutenant-Colonel Augustus Warburton, in charge – but with no instructions of any kind.

He couldn't get the Indians out of his mind. Their presence haunted him. The promises wrung from him at the council obsessed him. Tecumseh's taunts stung.

There was something more. His own superiors had stressed again and again the necessity of keeping on good terms with the tribes. They knew that without the Indians the war would have already been lost.

Procter had been ordered to keep the Indians happy "by any means in your power," and to promise them mountains of presents if they would only follow the army.

There was another fear. What if the Indians did defect? Would they fall upon the British, destroy the army, and swell the ranks of the invaders?

And so Procter was caught in a trap. If he lost his native allies he would be blamed; but if Tecumseh remained his ally, Procter wasn't really in charge. He sent his engineering officer upstream to the forks of the Thames, at the community of Chatham. The officer reported that this was not the best place to make the promised stand. But something had to be done.

Finally Procter selected Moraviantown (near the present community of Thamesville), twenty-six miles (41.6 km) farther upstream – a slightly better position.

Procter's intentions were clear. The army would stand and fight at Moraviantown, and not at the forks of the Thames. So, Henry Procter would always be able to say he had kept his promise to Tecumseh. But somehow, in his haste, he didn't get around to informing Lieutenant-Colonel Warburton, who was leading the army up the valley.

The British had abandoned Detroit, and with it control of all American territory captured the previous year. Now with the army back on Canadian soil, fleeing up the Thames Valley with Harrison close behind, another American force was also heading for Canada. Twelve hundred mounted Kentucky riflemen galloped along the Detroit road to help reinforce Harrison's invasion army. Their leader was a fiery young congressman, Colonel Richard Mentor Johnson.

Johnson, a handsome, stocky figure with a shock of auburn hair, had made a name for himself as an eloquent politician. He was the first native-born Kentuckian to be elected to both the state legislature and the federal congress. He was also a leading member of the group of War Hawks who had goaded the United States into declaring war on Canada in 1812.

Like so many of his colleagues, Johnson was reared on tales of Indian attacks. His family were all Indian-fighters. Unlike the New Englanders and the Pennsylvanians, the Kentuckians regarded the invasion of Canada as a holy war, "a second revolution as important as the first," in Johnson's words. It was also seen as a war of conquest.

Johnson made no bones about his belief that the English should be driven from the New World. "I shall never die contented until I see … her territories incorporated with the United States," he said.

That, of course, had not been the original intention of the Americans when they invaded Canada. They were simply infuriated because, although the United States had not taken sides during the Napoleonic Wars, the English had insisted on mounting a blockade to prevent American ships bringing supplies into French ports.

Angered by the British, but unable to attack them across three thousand miles (4,800 km) of Atlantic water, they decided instead to give Britain's main colony – Canada – a bloody nose. But the war had been going on for a year and that hadn't happened.

Recruits flocked to Johnson's banner – veterans of the American Revolution, former Indian-fighters, and young men raised on tales of adventure. They had all made their wills and had resolved never to return to Kentucky unless they came back as conquerors. The captain of the first battalion, Robert McAfee, was one who foresaw the shores of Lake Erie becoming the richest and most important section of the United States. "It is necessary that Canada should be ours," he wrote in his journal.

Johnson and his brother, James, had fifteen hundred six-month volunteers under their command. Each man was decked out in a blue hunting shirt with a red belt and blue pantaloons, also fringed with red. They were armed with pistols, swords, hunting knives, tomahawks, muskets, and Kentucky squirrel rifles.

Ever since mid-May, these men had been herded through the wilderness for more than twelve hundred miles (about 2,000 km) without once firing a shot at the enemy. They longed for action, and now at last it seemed they could smell it.

Johnson could hardly wait to get at Procter, whom he called a "monster," because Procter's Indians had massacred the Kentucky forces at the Battle of Frenchtown on the southwestern shore of Lake Erie the previous autumn. His men were just as eager. Off they rode toward Detroit, swimming their horses across the little streams, on the lookout for hostile Indians. The news of the British withdrawal excited them.

On the afternoon of September 30, they reached their objective. The entire population of Detroit turned out to greet them. The governor of Kentucky himself, old Isaac Shelby, had, at Harrison's request, brought some two thousand eager volunteers to swell the ranks of the invading army.

Johnson now learned to his surprise that Procter had abandoned Amherstburg without fighting and that Harrison had already seized that fort. Harrison now had a force of five thousand men. Two thousand were regular soldiers. The rest were amateurs.

Harrison didn't expect to catch Procter, because the British had grabbed every horse in the country. It was all he could do to find a broken-down pony to carry the ageing Shelby along with the troops. But he expected and hoped that Procter would make a stand somewhere on the Thames. Harrison's greatest fear was that Procter *wouldn't* stop. The American general wanted to fight and thought he could win.

Shelby hadn't been able to resist Harrison's request that he come along. He was sixty-three years old, paunchy and double-chinned, with close-cropped white hair. But he commanded the respect of the Kentucky soldiers, who called him Old King's Mountain after his memorable victory at that place during the Revolutionary war in 1780.

Harrison wanted Shelby's opinion: should the army pursue Procter by land up the Thames Valley, or should the troops be carried by boat to Long Point, along the lake, and then march in by the Long Point road? Shelby believed Procter could be overtaken by land. Harrison's council of war agreed.

Harrison decided to take thirty-five hundred men up the

Thames, leaving seven hundred behind to hold Detroit. Johnson's mounted volunteers would be in the lead. The rest, who had left their knapsacks and blankets on an island in the river, would follow.

But Harrison had real trouble persuading any Kentuckian to stay on the American side of the river. They considered it an insult to be left behind. In the end he had to conscript them to hold Detroit.

On the other hand, the Pennsylvania militia stood on their constitutional right not to fight outside the territory of the United States.

"I believe the boys are not willing to go, General," one of their captains told him.

"The boys, eh?" Harrison remarked sarcastically. "I believe some of the officers *too* are not willing to go. Thank God I have Kentuckians enough to go without you."

He knew that speed was all important. Shelby kept pointing out that "if we desire to overtake the enemy, we must do more than he does, by early and enforced marches."

And so at dawn on October 2, as Procter continued to dawdle, the Americans pushed forward, sometimes at a half-run to keep up with the mounted men. Johnson asked Harrison if he could ride ahead in search of the British rearguard, and Harrison agreed. But he added a word of caution: he was afraid of the Indians.

"Go, Colonel, but remember discipline. Be cautious, sir, as well as brave and active, as I know you all are."

Off went Johnson at the head of a group of volunteers. Not far from the Thames, they captured six British soldiers who told them that Procter's army was only fifteen miles (24 km) above the mouth of the river. It was nearly sunset, but when the regiment heard that, it was determined to move at once. In one day Harrison's army had marched twenty-five miles (40 km).

The troops set off again at dawn. Only three gunboats could get up the shallow and winding Thames. Harrison figured Procter didn't know the speed he was moving at, because Procter hadn't bothered to destroy any of the bridges to hold up the American advance.

That afternoon the army captured a British lieutenant and eleven dragoons. Now Harrison learned that the British had no knowledge of his advance.

By evening, his army was camped ten miles (16 km) up the river and just four miles (6.4 km) below Matthew Dolsen's farm at Dover, from which the British had only just departed. It had taken Procter five days to make the journey from Sandwich. Harrison managed to cover the same ground in less than half the time.

Chapter Four

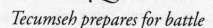

Tecumseh prepares for battle

AUGUSTUS WARBURTON, PROCTER'S second-in-command, was confused and perplexed. He had no idea what he was to do, because his commander hadn't told him. He had learned that the Americans were on the march a few miles downstream. His own men had reached the place where Procter had decided to make a stand, but now Procter had changed his mind and rushed up the river to Moraviantown, having apparently decided to meet the enemy there.

Captain William Crowther had a problem too. Procter had ordered him to fortify Dover, and Crowther wanted to throw up a temporary gun battery, cut loopholes in the log buildings, and dig trenches. But all the tools had been sent on to Bowles's farm seven miles (11 km) upriver. There were no wagons or boats to bring them back, and Crowther was unable to follow his orders.

It was too late anyway. Tecumseh was across the river on the *south* bank, and he insisted on moving three miles (4.8 km) upstream to Chatham, at the forks. It was there that Procter had originally promised to make a stand and, if necessary, lay his bones with those of the Indians. But again, he had neglected to tell Tecumseh of his change of plan.

Warburton wanted to keep the Indians on the British side, and so followed Tecumseh. The army, which had lingered at Dolsen's farm for two days waiting for Procter, moved three miles (4.8 km) to Chatham and stopped again. It was Tecumseh – not Procter, not Warburton – who was calling the tune.

The Shawnee war chief was in a fury; there were no fortifications at Chatham. Procter had betrayed him – or so he believed. Half his force had left, headed by Chief Walk-in-the-Water of the senior tribe of Wyandot.

Now Matthew Elliott, his life threatened by the angry natives, crossed the river and urged Warburton to stand and fight at Chatham.

"I will not, by God, sacrifice myself," he declared in tears.

Warburton asked Elliott to tell Tecumseh that he would try to keep Procter's promise and make a stand on any ground of the Indians' choosing. He had already sent two messages to Procter, warning him that the enemy was closing in and explaining that he had moved forward to Chatham. But Procter went on to Moraviantown regardless, after sending his wife off to safety at Burlington Heights.

The Indians were angered at Procter's absence. Tecumseh's brother, the Prophet, said he would personally like to tear off the general's epaulettes, because he wasn't fit to wear them. The army, too, was disturbed. Mutiny was in the air.

There was talk of Warburton taking over from Procter. But Warburton would have none of that. Major Adam Muir of the rearguard declared that Procter ought to be hanged for being away and Warburton hanged for shirking his responsibility.

With the American army at his heels, Warburton got two messages on the morning of October 4. The first came from Procter, announcing he would return to join the troops. The second, from Tecumseh, told him that the Indians had decided to retire to Moraviantown.

Warburton waited until ten in the morning – but still no Procter. He could hear shots across the river: the Indians skirmishing with the enemy. Just as he set his troops in motion he got another message from Procter, ordering him to move a few miles upriver to Bowles's farm. The column moved slowly, held up often by Indian women who forced it to halt time after time, to let them pass by.

Bowles's was as far as the boats could go; the river above was too shallow. There, Warburton finally met up with his general, who was already giving orders to destroy all the stores – guns, shells, cord, cable, naval equipment. In short, the long shuttle by boat from Amherstburg, which had held up the withdrawal, had been for nothing. Procter even ordered two gunboats sunk in the river to slow down the American progress.

By eight that evening, the forward troops had reached

Lemuel Sherman's farm, about four miles (6.4 km) from Moraviantown. There they halted for the night. Ovens were built, and orders were given for bread to be baked. But there was no bread: the bakers said they had to look after their families first. And so, footsore, exhausted, and half-starved, with their morale at its lowest ebb, the men subsisted on whatever bread they had saved from the last issue at Dolsen's.

Tecumseh, meanwhile, fought a rearguard action at the forks of the Thames, near Chatham. His followers tore the planks off the bridge at McGregor's Creek, and when Harrison's forward scouts, under a veteran frontiersman, William Whitley, tried to cross on what was left of the bridge, the natives opened fire from their hiding places in the woods.

Whitley, a sixty-three-year-old Indian-fighter and Kentucky pioneer, had insisted on marching as a private soldier under Harrison, accompanied by two black servants. As the Indians fired, he toppled off the muddy timbers and fell twelve feet (3.6 m) into the water, but he managed to swim ashore, gripping his silver-mounted rifle. The Indians were driven off with shots from two six-pounder (2.7 kg) cannons. The bridge was repaired, and the Americans pushed on.

Tecumseh reached Christopher Arnold's mill, twelve miles (19 km) upriver from the forks, that evening. Arnold, a militia captain, was already a friend of Tecumseh from an earlier encounter, and he offered him dinner and a bed. But he was worried about his mill: the Indians had already burned McGregor's. Tecumseh promised it would be spared, for he saw no point in useless destruction. With the other mill gone, the white settlers would have to depend on this one.

Fact mingles with myth in the reports of those last hours as Tecumseh prepared for battle. Those whose paths crossed his would always remember what was done and what was said, and they would hand it down years later to their sons and grandsons.

Young Johnny Toll, playing along the riverbank near McGregor's Creek, would never forget the hazel-eyed Shawnee who warned him, "Boy, run away home at once. The soldiers are coming. There is war and you might get hurt."

Sixteen-year-old Abraham Holmes would always remember the sight of the Shawnee war chief standing near the Arnold mill on the morning of October 5, his hand at the head of his white pony. What a scene that was: the tall figure dressed in buckskin from neck to knees, a sash at his waist, his headdress adorned with ostrich plumes, waiting until the last of his men had passed the mill and was safe. Holmes was so impressed he would name his first-born son Tecumseh.

Years later, Christopher Arnold would describe the same scene to his grandson, Thaddeus. Arnold remembered standing by the mill dam, waiting to spot the American vanguard. It was agreed he would signal its arrival by throwing up a shovelful of earth. But Tecumseh's eyes were sharper. He was on his horse, dashing off at full speed after the first glimpse of Harrison's scouts. At the farm of Arnold's brother-in-law, he stopped to perform a small act of charity, tossing a sack of Arnold's flour at the front door to sustain the family, who had run out of bread.

Lemuel Sherman's sixteen-year-old son, David, and a friend were driving cows through a swamp when they came upon Tecumseh, seated on a log, two pistols in his belt. The Shawnee chief asked young Sherman whose boy he was, and, on hearing that his father was a militiaman in Procter's army, told him, "Don't let the Americans know your father is in the army or they'll burn your house. Go back and stay home, for there will be a fight here soon."

Years later, when David Sherman had become a wealthy landowner, he laid out part of his property as a village and named it Tecumseh.

Billy Caldwell, the half-caste son of the Indian Department's Colonel William Caldwell, would always remember Tecumseh's fatalistic remark to some of his chiefs:

"Brother warriors, we are about to enter an engagement from which I shall not return. My body will remain on the field of battle."

Long before, when he was fifteen, facing his first musket fire against the Kentuckians, when his life stretched before him like a river without end, Tecumseh had feared death and run from the field. Now he seemed to welcome it because he had no further reason to live.

Young David Sherman and a friend encounter Tecumseh in the swamp.

Word had also reached him that the one real love of his life, Rebecca Galloway, had married. It was she who had introduced him to English literature. There had been other women and other wives (he had treated them all with disdain), but this sixteen-year-old daughter of an Ohio frontiersman was different. She spoke his language, taught him English, introduced him to the Bible, Alexander the Great, and Shakespeare's plays. He fell in love with her and brought her gifts – a silver comb, a birchbark canoe, furs, and deer meat.

He asked for her hand in marriage, offering her thirty silver brooches, and, so it was was said, she was ready to accept. However, she insisted he give up Indian life and adopt white customs and dress. But Tecumseh could not bring himself to adopt a course that would cost him the respect of his people. And so, reluctantly, they parted, never to meet again.

Now he was single. His last wife, White Wing, a Shawnee whom he had married in 1802, parted from him in 1807. There would be no more women in his life. He was wedded to an ideal.

Rebecca was part of a dead past, a dream that would not come true, like his own shattered dream of a united Indian nation.

In some ways, Tecumseh seems more Christian than the Christians, with his hatred of senseless violence and torture. He was considerate of others, chivalrous, moral, and, in his struggle for his people's existence, totally selfless. But he intended to go into battle as a pagan, daubed with his customary black paint, swinging his hatchet, screaming his war cry, remembering always the example of his elder brother, Cheeseekau, the father figure who brought him up and who in the end met death gloriously, attacking a Kentucky fort, expressing the joy he felt at dying – not like an old woman at home, but on a field of conflict, where the fowls of the air would pick his bones.

Chapter Five

~

Procter makes a stand

SINCE LEAVING DOLSEN'S, PROCTER'S TROOPS had had no rations. When they reached Lemuel Sherman's farm on the upper Thames, they were about to enjoy their first meal in twenty-four hours when the order came to pack up and march. The Americans were only a short distance behind them.

Some cattle had already been butchered, but there was no time to cook the beef and not a pan in which to roast it. And there was no bread. Some of the men stuffed raw meat into their mouths, or munched away on whatever crust they could still find from the last issue. The rest went hungry.

There was worse news. The Americans had seized all the British boats, capturing the extra ammunition, tools, and stores. The only cartridges the troops now had were in their own pouches. The officers tried to keep that information from their men.

The army marched two and a half miles (4 km). Procter appeared and brought it to a halt. Here, with the river on his left and a heavy marsh on his right, in a light wood of beech, maple, and oak, he had determined to make his stand.

It wasn't a bad position. His left flank was resting on the high bank of the river. That meant the enemy could not turn it. His right was protected by the marsh. He expected the Americans to advance down the road that cut through the left of his position. He planted his only gun – a six-pounder (2.7 kg) – at this point to rake the pathway.

He put the regulars on the left to hold the flank. The militia would form a line on the right. Beyond the militia, separated by a small swamp, would be Tecumseh's warriors.

Procter might have chosen to make his stand farther upstream, in the heights above Moraviantown. There, his position would have been protected by a deep ravine and the hundred log huts of the Christian Delaware Indians, who had lived here with their Moravian missionary since fleeing Ohio in 1792. It was to that village that Procter brought his main guns and supplies.

Why had he changed his plans so suddenly? It was the Indians who dictated the battle again. It was not their style to fight in the open plain, so Procter had no choice but to listen to them.

The tactics were simple. The British would hold the left, while the Indians, moving like a door on a hinge, would creep forward through the thicker forest on the right to attack Harrison's flank.

But there were problems. The worst was morale. The

troops were slouching about, sitting on logs and stumps. They had already been turned around once, marched forward and then back again for some sixty paces, grumbling about "doing neither one thing or another." An hour passed before they were brought to their feet and told to form a line.

There was another problem. Procter had only six hundred men – not enough to stand shoulder to shoulder in the accepted fashion. In those days of musket warfare, men did not spread out, nor did they aim their weapons at any particular object. They were drilled to stand as close together as possible and fire all their muskets at the opposing force. This withering fire – a cloud of musket balls aimed in the general direction of the enemy – had worked well on the European plains.

But now the line developed into a series of clusters as the troops tried to hide behind the trees. Apparently nobody thought of building any sort of bulwark – trenches, mounds of earth, barricades of logs and branches – that might stop the enemy's cavalry. And nobody noticed that on the British side of the line there wasn't any underbrush. But what could they do? All the shovels, axes, and entrenching tools had already been lost to the enemy.

The troops stood in position for two and a half hours, patiently waiting for the Americans to appear. They were weak from hunger and exhausted from the events of past week. They hadn't been paid for six months and were so poor they couldn't even afford soap. Their clothes were in rags. They were short of greatcoats and blankets. They were overworked and gloomy. Some had been on garrison duty far away from their homes in England for a decade. They could not see through the curtain of trees, but they heard rumours that Harrison had ten thousand men advancing to the attack.

And then there was Procter. Many of his men believed he was more interested in saving his wife and family than in saving them. Many believed they were about to be cut to pieces and sacrificed for nothing. And so they waited – and that wait seemed an eternity.

Tecumseh rode down the ragged line, clasping the hands of the officers, and murmuring encouragement in his own language. He had a special greeting for young John Richardson, whom he had known since childhood. Richardson noted the fringed deerskin ornamented with stained porcupine quills, the ostrich feathers, and, most of all, the dark, lively features and the flashing hazel eyes.

Whenever, in the future, John Richardson thought of Tecumseh – and he thought of him often – that picture would remain: the tall, sturdy chief on the white pony, who seemed now to be in such high spirits, who genially told Procter to urge his men to be stout-hearted and to take care the Long Knives did not seize the big cannon.

Tecumseh greets John Richardson on the line of battle.

Chapter Six

The Battle of the Thames

Harrison, having destroyed all the British gunboats and supplies, crossed the Thames in order to reach the right bank, along which the British had been retreating. The water was so deep the men hesitated until Harrison's aide, the naval commander Oliver Hazard Perry, rode through the crowd, shouted to a foot soldier to climb on behind, and dashed into the stream, calling on Colonel Johnson's mounted volunteers to follow.

In that way, with the aid of several abandoned canoes and keelboats, the three thousand foot soldiers were moved across the river in forty-five minutes.

William Whitley, the veteran scout, saw an Indian on the opposite bank and shot him. He swam his horse back across and scalped the corpse. "This is the thirteenth scalp I have taken," he told a friend, "and I'll have another by night or lose my own."

The Americans formed up on the right bank. A spy reported the British not far ahead, aiming for Moravian-town. Harrison rode up to Johnson and told him that the foot soldiers wouldn't be fast enough to overtake Procter until late in the day. He wanted Johnson to push his mounted regiment forward to stop the British retreat. "If you cannot compel them to stop with an engagement, why FIGHT them, but do not venture too much," Harrison ordered.

Johnson moved his men forward at a trot. A captured French-Canadian soldier told him that eight hundred men, supported by fourteen hundred Indians, lay ahead. Johnson, though apparently outnumbered, had no intention of retreating. But Procter did not attack. The two armies remained within view of one another – no more than a few hundred yards apart – motionless, waiting.

A quarter of an hour went by. Harrison arrived with his troops – eleven regiments supported by artillery, stretching back for three miles (4.8 km) – and held a council of war on horseback. At once he saw that Procter had a good position and realized that the British would use the Indians on the edge of the swamp to get around his flanks. That, he had to prevent at all costs.

His strategy was to hold the Indians back with a strong force on his left and attack the British line with a bayonet charge through the woods. At the same time, Johnson's mounted men would splash through the swamp that separated the British from the Indians and attack Tecumseh's tribesmen.

It took him an hour and a half to form up his troops. The British, peering through the oaks and beeches and the brilliant sugar maples, could catch only glimpses of the enemy three hundred yards (270 m) away. The Americans had a better view of the British in their scarlet jackets.

Now Johnson sent a man forward to look at the swamp and realized that it was impassable. Harrison's tactics wouldn't work.

Harrison wanted him to retire to the rear and form a reserve, but Johnson had another idea. "General Harrison, permit me to charge the enemy and the battle will be won in thirty minutes," he said. He meant the British on his right, and not the Indians, separated by the swamp on his left.

Harrison looked over the field. He could see that the British redcoats were spread out in open formation, not shoulder to shoulder. There were gaps between the clusters of men. The woods were thick with trees, but there wasn't much underbrush. And he knew that Johnson had trained his men to ride through the forests of Ohio, firing cartridges to get the horses used to the sound of guns. Most of them were expert marksmen, having ridden horseback since childhood.

"Damn them! Charge them!" cried Harrison, and he changed the order of battle on the spot. He was convinced that these unusual tactics would catch the British unprepared.

Now one of Johnson's scouts came back with welcome news. He had found a way through the swamp. It wouldn't be easy, for the ground was bad. Johnson turned to his brother, James: "Brother, take my place at the head of the first battalion. I will cross the swamp and fight the Indians at the head of the second battalion." He explained his reason: "You have a family, I have none." And so the younger brother would attack the British on the right, while the other Johnson would take his chances in the swamp.

A brief lull followed. One of Harrison's colonels rode out in front of his regiment and shouted, "Boys, we must either whip the British and Indians or they will kill and scalp every one of us. We cannot escape if we lose. Let us all die on the field or conquer."

Once again, Procter had bungled. He had repeatedly threatened that he couldn't control the Indians and that if the Americans attacked him they would be massacred by the tribesmen. Now the Americans believed him and were prepared, if necessary, for a suicidal attack.

The bugle sounded a charge. Seated on his horse halfway between the British lines, Procter heard the sound and asked what it meant. His brigade major told him it was the advance.

An Indian scout fired his musket, and without orders the entire British front line discharged their ragged volley at the advancing horsemen. The horses recoiled in confusion.

Procter was desperate to put his six-pound (2.7 kg) cannon into effect. "Damn that gun. Why doesn't it fire?" he said.

But the British horses had been so startled by the gunfire that they reared back. They became entangled in the trees and dragged the cannon away with them.

James Johnson rallied his men and charged forward as a second line of British defenders opened fire. "Charge them, my brave Kentuckians!" Harrison cried, as the volunteers dashed forward, yelling and shouting. They hit the left of the British line, which crumbled.

"Stop, 41st, stop!" Procter shouted. "What are you about? For shame. For shame on you!"

The force of the cavalry charge had taken Johnson's horsemen right through both British lines. Now they wheeled around to their left to roll up the British right, which was still holding.

"For God's sake, men, stand and fight!" cried a sergeant of the 41st.

Not far away stood John Richardson, age sixteen, but already the survivor of three bloody skirmishes. A fellow officer pointed at one of the mounted riflemen taking aim at a British foot soldier. Richardson raised his musket, leaned against a tree for support, and dropped the mounted man from his horse.

Richardson now saw one of the Delaware chiefs throw a tomahawk at a wounded Kentuckian with such force that it opened his skull and killed him instantly. The Delaware pulled out the hatchet and scalped the man. That grisly scene was no sooner over than the firing in the woods on Richardson's left ended suddenly. The order came to retreat.

Procter was preparing to make off. His gun crew had fled. The Americans had seized the six-pounder (2.7 kg).

John Hall, his brigade major, warned him that unless they moved swiftly they would both be shot.

"Clear the road!" Hall cried. But the road was clogged with fleeing British. He suggested to the general they take to the woods. Procter, stunned by the suddenness of defeat, didn't appear to hear him. No more than five minutes had passed since Harrison's bugle sounded.

"This way, general, this way," said Hall patiently, like a parent leading a child. The general followed obediently.

"Do you not think we can join the Indians?" he asked. Tecumseh's force on the right of the shattered British line was still fighting furiously. But James Johnson's charge had cut Procter's army in two, and there was no way of reaching the Indians because there were mounted Americans between the Indian and British forces.

Off Procter went, riding as fast as he could, with the Americans in hot pursuit. He knew the Kentucky volunteers' reputation. For all he knew they might skin him alive if they caught him. So he galloped away from the battle as fast as he could, with the sounds of Tecumseh's Indians, still holding, echoing in his ears.

As James Johnson's men drove the British before them, his brother's battalion plunged through the decaying trees and willows of the small swamp that separated the Indians from their white allies. Richard Johnson's plan was brutal. He called for volunteers, for what was in effect a suicide squad – known in both armies as the Forlorn Hope. This screen of twenty bold men was instructed to ride ahead of the main body to attract the Indians' fire. Then, while the tribesmen were reloading, the main body would sweep down on them.

There was no problem with volunteers. The grizzled Whitley, a fresh scalp still dangling from his belt, would lead the Forlorn Hope, and Johnson would ride with them. Off they plunged through the water and mud into a hail of musket balls. Now, above the noise of battle, another sound was heard – clear, authoritative, almost melodic – the golden voice of Tecumseh urging his followers on to victory.

Johnson's tactic was working. The Indians had concentrated all their fire on the Forlorn Hope, killing fifteen of

Tecumseh's last battle, October 5, 1813.

the twenty, including William Whitley. But Johnson faced a problem. The mud of the swamp had risen to the horses' bellies. His men could not charge.

Bleeding from four wounds, Johnson ordered his followers to dismount and attack. An Indian behind a tree fired, and the ball struck a knuckle of Johnson's left hand, coming out just above the wrist. The Indian advanced, his tomahawk raised, but Johnson, who had loaded his pistol with one ball and three buckshot, drew his weapon and fired, killing the man instantly. Not far away lay Whitley's corpse, riddled with musket balls.

Beyond the protecting curtain of gunsmoke, the battle with the Indians raged on. Word had spread that Richard

Johnson was dead. An old friend, Major W. T. Barry, rode up from the rear to examine the corpse, but met a group of soldiers carrying the colonel back in a blanket.

"I will not die, Barry," Johnson assured him. "I am mightily cut to pieces, but I think my vitals have escaped." One day he would become vice-president of the United States.

The noise of the battle behind him continued to sound in his ears as the Americans pressed forward through the trees. The volume rose. The Kentuckians were shouting their battle cry. The Indians were shrieking and whooping. Wounded men were groaning and screaming. Horses were neighing and whinnying. The sound of musket and rifle fire shattered ear drums, as bugles sounded and cannon fired.

The smoke of battle lay thickly over forest and swamp, making ghosts of the dim, painted figures of Tecumseh's men, who would appear for an instant from the cover of trees to fire a weapon or hurl a tomahawk and then vanish into the gloom. They did not seem to be real to the Americans, for their faces could only be seen in death.

Who were the leaders, and who were the followers? One man, the Kentuckians knew, was in charge. They could hear Tecumseh's terrible battle cry piercing the ragged wall of sound. For five years they had heard its echo, ever since he had first made his presence felt in the Northwest.

Yet that presence had always been ghostly; no Kentuckian on the field that day – no white American, in fact, except for Harrison – had ever seen the Shawnee chief or heard his voice until this moment. He was a figure of legend, his origins clouded in myth, his image a reflection of other men's ideas. Johnson's riders were tantalized by his invisibility.

And then, suddenly, came a subtle change in the sound. Private Charles Wickliffe, who had been timing the battle, noticed it. Something was missing. Wickliffe groped for an answer and then came to realize that he could no longer hear that one clear cry. The voice of Tecumseh urging on his followers had been stilled. The Shawnee had fallen.

The absence of that sound was as clear as a bugle call. Suddenly the battle was over. The Indians withdrew through the underbrush, leaving the field to the Americans. As the firing trailed off, Wickliffe took out his watch. Exactly fifty-five minutes had elapsed since Harrison ordered the first charge. As the late afternoon shadows gathered, a pall rose over the bodies of the slain.

But one corpse was missing. Elusive in life, Tecumseh remained invisible in death. No white man had ever been allowed to draw his likeness. No white man would ever display or mutilate his body. No headstone, marker, or monument would identify his resting place. His people had spirited him away to a spot where no stranger would ever find him – his earthly clay, like his own forlorn hope, buried forever in a secret grave.

Chapter Seven

~ The legend begins

FLEEING FROM JAMES JOHNSON'S RIDERS, even as the battle still raged, young John Richardson charged through the woods with his comrades and lost his way. He found himself unexpectedly on the road, now clogged with wagons, discarded stores and clothing, women and children.

Five hundred yards (450 m) to his right he saw the main body of the regiment, disarmed and surrounded by the enemy. Acting on instinct, he and the others turned left, only to run into a body of American cavalry, the men walking their horses.

Their leader, a stout, elderly officer dressed like his men in a Kentucky hunting jacket, saw them, galloped forward, waved his sword, and shouted in a commanding voice:

"Surrender, surrender! It's no use. It's no use resisting. All your people are taken and you'd better surrender."

That was Shelby. Richardson, whose attitude towards all Americans was snobbishly British-Canadian, thought him a vulgar man, who looked more like one of the army's wagon drivers than the governor of a state. Certainly, he didn't look a bit like a chief magistrate in one of His Majesty's provinces.

Richardson quickly buried his musket in the deep mud – to keep it from the enemy – and gave up. As the troops passed by, one tall Kentuckian glanced over at the little teenager and said, "Well, I guess now, you tarnation little Britisher, who'd calculate to see such a bit of chap as you here?" Richardson would never forget that remark, which showed the difference in the languages of the two English-speaking peoples who shared the continent.

Meanwhile, Major Eleazer Wood was in full pursuit of Procter. But the general escaped, stopping only briefly at Moraviantown and then moving on to Ancaster, so tired he couldn't even write a coherent account of the day's action that evening. Wood had to be content with capturing his carriage, containing his sword, hat, trunk, and all his personal papers, including a packet of letters from his wife.

Moraviantown's single street was clogged with wagons, horses, and half-starved Kentuckians. The missionary's wife, Mrs. Schall, worked all night baking bread for the troops, some of whom pounced on the dough and ate it before it went into the oven. Others upset all the beehives, scrambling for the honey, and ravaged the garden for vegetables, which they devoured raw.

Richardson and the other prisoners fared better. Squatting around a campfire in the forest, they were fed pieces of meat toasted on skewers by Harrison's aides, who told the

British that they were sorry to hear of the death of the much-admired Tecumseh.

Now began the long argument over the Shawnee's death. Who had killed Tecumseh? Some said Whitley, whose body was found near that of an Indian chief. Others, including Shelby, thought that a private from Lincoln County had shot him. Another group insisted that the Indian killed by Richard Johnson was Tecumseh. That would form the most colourful feature of Johnson's campaign for the vice-presidency.

But nobody knew or would ever know how Tecumseh fell. Only two men on the American side knew what he looked like – Harrison, his old enemy, and Anthony Shane, the mixed-blood interpreter who had known him as a boy. Neither was able to say with certainty that any of the bodies in the field looked like the Indian leader.

The morning after the battle, David Sherman, the boy who had encountered Tecumseh in the swamp, found one of his rifled flintlock pistols on the field. That same day, Chris Arnold came upon a group of Kentuckians skinning the body of an Indian to make souvenir razor strops.

"That's not Tecumseh," Arnold told them.

"I guess when we get back to Kentucky they will not know his skin from Tecumseh's," they replied.

In death as in life, the Shawnee war chief inspired myth. There were some who believed he had not been killed at all but merely wounded, and that he would return to lead his people to victory. That was a wistful hope. But "skeletons" of Tecumseh would turn up in the future. "Authentic" graves would be identified and then rejected. Yet the facts of his death and his burial remain as elusive as those of his birth almost half a century before.

John Richardson was moved back to the Detroit River with six hundred other prisoners. Luckily for him, his grandfather, John Askin, of Amherstburg, had a son-in-law, Elijah Brush, who was an American military colonel at Detroit. Askin wrote to his daughter's husband, telling him to look after his grandson. As a result, Richardson, instead of being sent up the Maumee River with the others, was taken to Put-in Bay by gunboat. There, he ran into his own father, Dr. Robert Richardson, an army surgeon captured by Perry.

The double victories, first on Lake Erie and now on the Thames, tipped the scales of war. For all practical purposes, the conflict on the Detroit frontier was ended. The British expected Harrison to follow up his victory and so fell into a panic, destroying stocks of arms and supplies as they retreated to the protection of Burlington Heights, above the present site of Hamilton, Ontario. The army was in dreadful shape. Of eleven hundred men, eight hundred were sick, too ill to haul wagons up the hills or through the rivers of mud that passed for roads.

Now the British were prepared to let all of Upper Canada west of Kingston fall to the Americans. The Americans, however, could not maintain their momentum. Harrison's supply lines were stretched too far. The Thames Valley had been stripped of fodder, grain, and meat. His six-month volunteers were all clamouring to go home.

In the end, Harrison was a captive of his country's hand-to-mouth recruiting methods. He could not pursue the remnants of Procter's army as common sense dictated. Instead, he had to move back down the Thames River, try to hold on to Fort Amherstburg, and leave one of his brigadiers in charge of Detroit.

The war was by no means over; and neither side had yet won. The British still held a key outpost in the far west – the captured island of Michilimackinac, guarding the route to the fur country at the northern end of Lake Huron. It was essential that the Americans grab it. They should have been able to do so with their superior fleet, but the Canadian winter frustrated that plan.

In the United States victory bonfires lit up the sky. Songs were written for the occasion. Harrison was toasted at every table, and Congress struck a gold medal. It was this that rocketed Harrison to the presidency. An extraordinary number of those who fought with him also rose to high office.

For Henry Procter there was no praise. A court martial the following year found him guilty of negligence, of bungling the retreat, of errors in tactics and judgement. He was publicly reprimanded and suspended from rank and pay for six months.

If he had retreated promptly and without baggage, he might have saved his army. And yet it was the army he blamed for all his misfortunes – not himself. In his report of the battle and his testimony at the court martial, he threw all the responsibility of defeat on the shoulders of the men and officers serving under him. But in the end it was Procter's reputation that was tarnished and not that of his men.

To the Americans he would remain a monster, to the Canadians a coward. He was neither, merely a victim of circumstance, a brave but weak officer, capable enough except in moments of stress, unable to make the huge leap that distinguishes the outstanding leader from the run-of-the-mill: the quality of being able in moments of difficulty to rise above his own limitations. The prisoner of events beyond his control, he dallied until he was crushed. His career was ended.

He left the valley of the Thames in a shambles. Moraviantown was a smoking ruin, destroyed on Harrison's orders to prevent its being used as a British base. Bridges were broken, grist mills burned, grain destroyed, sawmills shattered. Indians and soldiers of both armies had plundered homes, slaughtered cattle, stolen private property.

And Tecumseh's dreamed-of confederacy – a union of all the tribes – was finally dead. In Detroit thirty-seven chiefs representing six tribes signed an armistice with Harrison, leaving their wives and children as hostages for their good intentions. The Americans didn't have enough to feed them, and so the women and children were seen grubbing in the streets for bones and rinds of pork thrown away by the soldiers. Rotting meat discarded in the river was retrieved and devoured. On the Canadian side, two thousand Indian women and children swarmed into Burlington Heights pleading for food.

Kentucky had been battling the Indians for half a century. Now the long struggle for possession of the Northwest was over. And that was the real significance of Harrison's victory. The proud tribes had been humbled. The Indian lands were ripe for the taking.

The personal struggle between Harrison and Tecumseh had all the elements of classic tragedy, and, as in classic tragedy, it is the fallen hero and not the victor whom history will remember.

Harrison died after a single month in office. It was his fate to be remembered as a one-month president, forever to be confused with his grandson Benjamin, a longer-lived President Harrison. But in death, as in life, there was only one Tecumseh. His last resting place, like so much of his career, is a mystery. But his memory will be forever green.

Index

mounted, 28, 32, 48, 53;
numbers of, 28, 30-32, 49;
Pennsylvania militia, 32;
and plundering, 63;
regular forces, 31;
uniforms, 30;
volunteers, disadvantages of,
20-21, 32, 62
Troops, British:
battle tactics of, 44-45;
condition of, 37, 45-46, 61;
41st Regiment, 25, 44, 52;
and illness, 61;
and Indians, 26, 44, 56, 49;
and lack of food and provisions,
20, 37, 43, 45;
and lack of weapons and
ammunition, 20, 43;
militia, 44;
numbers of, 14, 45, 49, 61;
and plundering, 63;
poor morale of, 20, 36, 37,
44-45, 46;
as prisoners, 33, 59;
surrender of, 58-59

UNITED STATES:
and control of Lake Erie, 20;

intentions of in invading
Canada, 29;
strategy of, 31-32, 48-50, 61-62;
see also Troops, American

VOLUNTEER ARMY,
DISADVANTAGES OF, 20-21, 32,
62

WABASH RIVER, 10
Walk-in-the-Water, Chief, 35
Warburton, Lieutenant-Colonel
Augustus, 27, 28, 34, 35-36
Wayne, General "Mad Anthony,"
16
Weapons:
bayonets, 16, 49;
Kentucky squirrel rifles, 30, 56;
muskets, 16, 30, 44, 56;
six-pounder cannons, 37, 44, 51,
52, 56;
tomahawks, 30, 52, 55, 56
White Wing, 41
Whitley, William, 37, 48, 54, 55,
60
Wickliffe, Private Charles, 57
Wood, Major Eleazer, 59
Wyandot band, 26, 35

Coming Soon

STEEL ACROSS THE SHIELD

The Canadian Shield splits Canada in two. A 1,500-kilometre barrier of rock and muskeg, it hampered settlers of the nineteenth century from having easy access to the fertile plains, rolling hills, and majestic mountains of western Canada. Hampered them, that is, until the mid-1880s when a railway was finally constructed across the Shield to Winnipeg, Manitoba.

Steel Across the Shield is the gripping story of how that railroad line was blasted from ancient rock and floated over vast swamps to connect with the ribbon of steel already being driven across the plains and over the mountains of Alberta and British Columbia. It's also the story of how this transcontinental railway was saved from seeming collapse at the very last moment by an armed rebellion in what is now the province of Saskatchewan.

Steel Across the Shield is another vivid instalment in Pierre Berton's informative, accessible series about the construction of the CPR and the settling of the Canadian West.